Better places to work

CABE and Llewelyn Davies Yeang

Commission for Architecture
and the Built Environment

llewelyn
davies yeang
architecture
planning
design

AtisReal

BRITISH PROPERTY
FEDERATION

Published by Thomas Telford Publishing, Thomas Telford Ltd, 1 Heron Quay, London E14 4JD. URL: www.thomastelford.com

Distributors for Thomas Telford books are

USA: ASCE Press, 1801 Alexander Bell Drive, Reston, VA 20191-4400, USA

Japan: Maruzen Co. Ltd, Book Department, 3–10 Nihonbashi 2-chome, Chuo-ku, Tokyo 103

Australia: DA Books and Journals, 648 Whitehorse Road, Mitcham 3132, Victoria

First published 2005

Also available from Thomas Telford Books

By design: better places to live. ISBN: 07277 3037 1

A catalogue record for this book is available from the British Library

ISBN: 0 7277 3398 2

Designed and typeset by Kneath Associates, Swansea

Printed and bound in Great Britain by Latimer Trend Ltd., Plymouth

Contents

Foreword

The best employers have long since recognised that a well designed and planned workplace can bring huge benefits. The 20th century saw major strides in terms of the functionality of workplaces – such as the assembly line or the open plan office – but often failed to create a place where workers felt valued. Now that employers are increasingly seeing their workers as their single biggest asset, and see a good quality environment as a key ingredient in attracting employees, the need for built environment professionals to create workplaces where people want to work becomes more and more vital to a successful economy. We are pleased that the Commission for Architecture and the Built Environment (CABE), the British Council for Offices (BCO) and the British Property Federation (BPF) have come together to produce this publication.

Recent reports by CABE have found that increased standards of design can have a significant positive effect upon the productivity of the occupants of workplaces. People who work in well designed and well located workplaces naturally feel more valued as employees and, as a result, are more productive and less likely to be thinking of moving on. Conversely, employers who provide badly designed and located workplaces are more likely to have a severely demoralised workforce and thus face significant recruitment and retention issues.

While there are examples of excellent workplace design from all eras across the country, many employees still spend nearly half their total waking hours in artificially illuminated boxes situated on soulless out of town trading estates. This is bad for workers and also bad for long term economic sustainability.

However, as the examples in this guide show, with a clear commitment from the employer and a favourable planning environment, it is possible to create better workplaces. This guide demonstrates that far from being in opposition, the needs of the employers and the economy, the local environment and the quality of life of the neighbouring communities can all be met by making workplaces better. This guide is concerned with how well designed workplaces can be delivered through the planning system. It explores issues around location, public realm, architecture and linkages, but not interior layouts of detailed specification. Excellent workplaces are places that perform their function efficiently, enhance the local environment and provide local employment in a place where people want to work. We should all be aiming to make these workplaces the rule rather than the exception.

John Sorrell
CABE Chairman

Simon Ward
BCO President

Ian Coull
President of BPF

CHAPTER 01

The need for better places to work

- Why good planning for workplaces is important
- About the guide

1.1 Why good planning for workplaces is important

We spend more time in our workplaces than any other place after our homes. However, compared with housing, we don't seem to give them nearly as much attention – as individuals or as those responsible for their planning and design. This needs to change.

Well designed, accessible and pleasant working environments are one of the key requirements of creating sustainable communities, as set out in The Sustainable Communities Plan 'Building for the Future'.

There are currently 582 million square metres of industrial and commercial floorspace in England and Wales. As Figure 1.1 shows, the amount of office and warehouse floorspace is rising at about 3% each year, although factory floorspace is decreasing slightly.

Given this overall growth it is important to get new development right. Poor planning and design risk a return to some of the mistakes of the past, such as:

- badly located sites, accessible only by car and excluding those without access to a car;
- low levels of density, representing an inefficient use of land and leading to:
  - car-dominated public spaces;
  - traffic generation;
  - inability to support a viable public transport service and a lack of facilities, such as leisure and recreation, for users of buildings;
- mono-use, leading to deserted places out of normal working hours and lack of natural surveillance, which in turn either encourages anti-social behaviour or excessive security arrangements;
- lack of adaptability leading to units quickly becoming obsolete;
- lack of, or poorly designed and maintained, landscaping leading to a low-quality environment.

Poorly located and designed places of work are not only bad for the wider environment, they are also bad for business. Evidence collated by and for CABE[1] shows that poor workplaces are:

- bad for business productivity and efficiency;
- bad for recruitment, retention and employee satisfaction;
- bad for the balance sheet – costing more over the lifetime of the building.

While much has been written about how to achieve well designed urban environments, for example By design (DETR/CABE, 2000), most literature produced on industrial and commercial development has been done by a few forward-thinking organisations in response to local development pressures. And much of that writing relates to the interior layouts of offices.

As a challenge and inspiration to everybody within the development industry, this guide draws on the lessons of success stories from around England to show how the planning for our workplaces can be improved for the benefit of all involved.

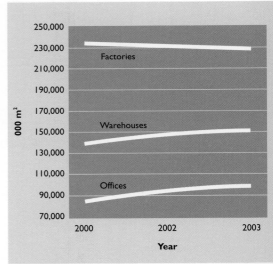

Fig 1.1 Change in floorspace by category 2000–2003. Source: ODPM

1.2 About the guide

Better places to work is concerned with those elements of the design and development of workplaces that the planning system can influence. So it explores issues around location, the public realm, architecture and linkages, for example, but not interior layouts or detailed specifications.

This guide has been prepared for the Commission for Architecture and the Built Environment (CABE), in partnership with the British Council for Offices (BCO) and British Property Federation (BPF), and is supported by the Office of the Deputy Prime Minister (ODPM).

The national policy context is provided within PPS1 (Delivering Sustainable Development), PPG4 (Industrial, Commercial Development and Small Firms), PPS6 (Planning for Town Centres) and PPG13 (Transport).

> Government planning policy, set out in PPS1: Delivering Sustainable Development, states that planning should facilitate and promote sustainable and inclusive patterns of urban and rural development by ensuring high-quality development through good and inclusive design. Planning authorities should plan positively for the achievement of high-quality and inclusive design for all development. PPS1 makes it clear that good design should contribute positively to making places better for people, and that design which is inappropriate in its context, or which fails to take the opportunities available for improving the character and quality of an area and the way it functions, should not be accepted.

By design – urban design in the planning system: towards better practice (DETR/CABE, 2000) sets out further guidance and good practice on achieving high-quality design; which is referred to in more detail in Chapter 2.1 of this guide.

Better places to work supports and builds on the principles of design set out in *By design*. It focuses on ten exemplar developments from around England and distils the lessons from the case studies to offer guidance to all those involved in all stages of the development process, from designers and developers through local planning authorities to property agents and all those who occupy business premises.

The guide relates to all developments where a role as a place of work is the primary reason people visit, such as factories, offices, warehouses, workshops and call centres. It does not specifically relate to locations where the primary function is not as a place of work, such as schools, hospitals or shops, even though these institutions are major employers.

The content of this guidance does not necessarily represent the views or policies of the Office of the Deputy Prime Minister.

1. See, for example, *The value of good design*, CABE, 2002, on www.cabe.org.uk and *Impact of Office design and business performance*, DEGW for CABE and the British Council for Offices, forthcoming 2005

Six principles of better places to work

2.1 Formulating the principles

Discussions with planners, designers, developers, occupiers and those responsible for procuring workplace developments, led to the identification of six principles that contribute to a better place to work and can be influenced through the planning system. A review of previous research on the topic and a wider urban design guidance also contributed to the development of the principles. Developments achieving planning permission, and successful workplaces in general, will exhibit many of these principles, and the best aim to meet all of them.

These principles, which are explained in more detail in the following section, are a direct interpretation of the characteristics that *By design* (DETR/CABE, 2000) identifies as being common to successful streets, spaces, villages, towns and cities. They are:

- character
- continuity and enclosure
- quality of the public realm
- ease of movement
- legibility
- adaptability
- diversity.

This means that there is a clear link between *Better places to work* and *By design*. The advice in *By design* remains relevant to the workplace context, but the guidance within this publication is much more focused on the particular requirements of the planning and design of workplaces that have specific requirements in areas such as:

- use of and take-up of space
- public access
- servicing
- procurement
- pollution
- need to be near markets.

The principles of better places to work:

Ease of movement and legibility
Workplaces that are located to be accessible by a wide range of transport modes, including foot, cycle, public transport and car.

Character, quality and continuity
Workplaces that exhibit a strong positive relationship with surrounding areas, services and facilities.

Diversity Workplaces that contribute to the vitality and viability of their locality by providing, adding to, and supporting a mix of complementary uses.

Sustainability Workplaces that minimise energy use through design, both during construction and in occupation.

Adaptability Workplaces that are able to accommodate changing requirements, including responding to changing market forces practically and cost effectively.

Management Workplaces that are designed to accommodate systematic management and maintenance regimes so that quality and consistency are maintained.

2.2 The principles

Ease of movement and legibility

Workplaces that are located to be accessible by a wide range of transport modes, including foot, cycle, public transport and car.

- Users can easily access a site, and find their way around the site without difficulty.
- The workplace is easily and conveniently accessible by public transport, reducing reliance on the car.
- The site is well laid out and carefully integrates pedestrian movement, vehicle movement and parking to create people-friendly public spaces.
- There are good-quality interchanges between transport modes nearby.
- There is a co-ordinated environment where the built form works with the transport network.
- Users can easily access services such as shops, cafés and banks.
- Locations outside urban centres pursue measures to reduce car use, such as provision for cycling, encouraging car-share, reducing parking spaces and providing bus links to public transport interchanges, articulated in a Green Travel Plan.
- Services and service access are sited in functional, unobtrusive, locations.

Character, quality and continuity

Workplaces that exhibit a strong positive relationship with surrounding areas, services and facilities.

- The design of the workplace contributes to, and is an integral part of, the quality of the wider public realm, sitting comfortably within the surrounding spaces, streets, buildings and communities.
- The workplace has a positive impact on the local economy.
- The workplace is a visually pleasing environment with a strong sense of place.
- Functional requirements such as parking ratios, highway requirements and building footprints are integrated into the creation of a successful place and are not allowed to predetermine design decisions.
- Materials and the detail of external spaces and buildings create a coherent and attractive whole.

Fig 2.1 Vodafone's UK headquarters in Newbury provides a legible environment for easy orientation

Fig 2.2 Cannon Avent's production facility in Glemsford, Suffolk uses glazing and curved walls in a successful reinterpretation of the industrial 'shed'

Diversity

Workplaces that contribute to the vitality and viability of their locality by providing a mix of complementary uses.

- The workplace provides an activity that diversifies but complements those already found in the local area.
- The design and layout of the workplace, along with planning conditions applied, negate the possibility of it being a 'bad neighbour'.
- A mix of uses on the site (for example, commercial, leisure, retail and residential development as well as office space) benefits both the workplace's users and the local area.

Sustainability

Workplaces that contribute to the achievement of sustainable development by minimising energy use through design, both during construction and in occupation.

- The location has been chosen with sustainability in mind, for example transport.
- The workplace is constructed to BRE Environmental Assessment Method (BREEAM) energy efficiency standards for offices and industrial premises (an assessment that includes consideration of health and well-being, energy, transport, water, materials and pollution–see www.breeam.org).
- Energy use and CO_2 emissions are minimised through design, including measures such as natural ventilation, orientation, energy recycling, passive solar design/natural day-lighting, grey water recycling and insulation.
- The building provides a healthy working environment.
- Sustainability is promoted through construction techniques, such as those that minimise waste, prevent pollution and protect wildlife and their habitats, use of local labour and local materials from sustainable sources.
- Biodiversity is conserved and enhanced, including recognising the value of existing landscape features.

Fig 2.3 Sheffield's Workstation forms part of a genuinely mixed-use development that includes a cinema, a crèche, exhibition space and a café

Fig 2.4 The Solar Office in Doxford, near Sunderland, was the first speculative office building to incorporate photovoltaic panels, and has adopted a holistic energy strategy

Adaptability

Workplaces that are able to accommodate changing requirements, including responding to changing market forces.

- The workplace has the ability to accommodate changing technological, economic, social and environmental requirements.
- The workplace has the capability of being altered or extended conveniently when necessary.
- The built structure can be easily converted from one use to another, for example office to residential and back again.
- The development allows for as many servicing and layout options as possible, enabling transience in terms of tenant turnover and changes in terms of work-setting change.

Management

Workplaces that are designed to accommodate systematic management and maintenance regimes so that quality and sustainability is maintained.

- Management and maintenance regimes are enforced so that quality is maintained.
- Public and communal space and landscaping is maintained and not allowed to fall into neglect.
- Green Travel Plans and other strategies are in place.
- The workplace continues to positively contribute to the charachter of the local area.

Fig 2.5 The Hothouse Railway arches, Hackney, a built form that can commonly be adapted for workplaces. New built element currently used as one open plan office but is designed to enable later subdivision into several smaller units.

Fig 2.6 Westbourne Studios in the Royal Borough of Kensington and Chelsea makes bicycles and electric cars available to tenants

CHAPTER 03

Key findings from the case studies

- **Introduction to the case studies**
- **Key findings**

3.1 Introduction to the case studies

Government policy requires a high standard of design and sustainable planning for all development. If we are to meet the challenge of providing better places to work, we must apply the principles discussed in Chapter 2.

Indeed, good workplaces, applying the principles introduced in the previous chapter, can be found all over the country. This guide introduces just ten of those workplaces. They have met the challenges faced in an imaginative, thoughtful and successful way. These are places that work for the developers, occupiers, customers and the wider local area. These are workplaces that mean business.

The case studies are included as role models and each provides lessons to be learnt. They are exemplars of what can be achieved and of the standard that local planning authorities, developers, designers and businesses should expect to see as the norm. They show what is possible when good design meets good planning. They are expected to inspire.

While none of the exemplar workplaces is perfect, they all demonstrate how the principles of better places to work discussed above can be achieved. Those principles are the starting point, the case studies their manifestation.

This chapter extracts the main lessons from these exemplar developments. It does this by first highlighting a number of recurrent themes, or findings, from the case studies. The following chapter adopts a 'how to' approach, suggesting some key steps that all those involved in the planning, design and development of workplaces would be expected to take.

The ten exemplar workplaces explored in Annex A are (in alphabetical order):

- **Capital One, Nottingham**: the UK headquarters and call centre of a financial company
- **Chiswick Park, London**: a business park in an urban context
- **The Custard Factory, Birmingham**: a mixed use development incorporating small offices and studios for the creative industries
- **Ercol Factory, Princes Risborough, Buckinghamshire**: a furniture factory
- **North Wiltshire District Council, Chippenham**: council offices, delivered by way of the Private Finance Initiative
- **One Central Square, Newcastle upon Tyne**: a multi-occupancy office block converted from a 1930s postal sorting office
- **One Piccadilly Gardens, Manchester**: a major speculative office development
- **The Printworks, Clitheroe, Lancashire**: an office block in a rural setting
- **3663, Langley Mill, Derbyshire**: a food processing and distribution depot
- **Wessex Water Operations Centre, near Bath**: head office and other facilities of a utility company

Fig 3.1 The quality of design of the Printworks, Clitheroe, enabled the development to achieve above average return in an area of limited demand

Fig 3.2 Architectural and landscape design are a large part of what makes Chiswick Park so marketable

3.2 Key findings

The review of the ten better places to work produced a number of key messages that arose repeatedly. As a broad guide, these are summarised in this section.

Good design is good business

Good design and careful planning make sound financial sense. A high-quality environment in which people work and customers visit can raise the profile of businesses, and carefully planned locations improve access to potential customers and markets. Providing a pleasant, professional and convenient place of work can also increase staff morale and satisfaction, which in turn can increase productivity and improve recruitment and retention. Good design also creates places that local people are proud to have within their neighbourhood.

Quality design leads to local economic development

A high-quality workplace can act as a catalyst for the regeneration of a wider area, creating and supporting diverse and successful neighbourhoods and places. It does this not just by providing employment for local people, but also by changing the character, mix of uses and amenities of an area. A successful, well designed workplace can attract more of the same, support transport facilities and lead to environmental improvement. It can transform perceptions and help to ensure economic well-being.

Fig 3.3 Birmingham's Custard Factory is the catalyst for the emergence of Digbeth as a cultural quarter

Fig 3.5 North Wiltshire District Council's offices in Chippenham succeeds on five of the six principles of a better place to work, evidence of a rounded approach to development

Fig 3.4 The development of One Piccadilly Gardens in Manchester included significant improvements to the surrounding public realm

Fig 3.6 Capital One's central Nottingham location is key to it also demonstrating five of the six principles

A holistic approach leads to better workplaces

Most successful developments in the case studies were those where a holistic approach had been taken, with consideration being given to as many of the principles of better places to work as possible. Projects strong on one or two principles, such as those relating to architectural design or sustainable construction, and deficient in others, such as those relating to context or accessibility, do not produce a satisfactory outcome. That said, examples of case studies demonstrating all of the principles are rare, leading to the conclusion that a more rigorous approach is desirable in planning for and allocating employment locations, including individual plots in business parks.

The oppurtunity to re-use developed land and existing buildings should be maximised

Previously developed land provides good opportunities for sustainable transport, integration into existing social infrastructure and mixing uses. In terms of sustainability, the conversion of existing premises and use of brownfield sites are almost always preferable to undeveloped greenfield locations.

Fig 3.7 The Custard Factory, Birmingham, is an imaginative and efficient re-use of existing buildings

Fig 3.8 The construction of 3663's Langley Mill depot on previously used urban land represents an emerging trend for warehousing

Transport choice leads to sustainability

The presence of a range of both public transport facilities and road access for private cars is a key success factor. It is desirable to enable staff, customers and suppliers to be able to make sustainable transport choices. Urban sites are usually better positioned to offer these choices.

Management and maintenance need to be considered at the planning stage

A strong management regime will be reflected in high standards of maintenance both of buildings and grounds, continuing effectiveness of energy-saving elements, implementation of travel plans (staff buses, facilities for cyclists, car sharing schemes) and staff welfare issues.

Fig 3.11 Chiswick Park's management is very proactive, for example making bicycles available for tenants

Fig 3.9 This view from Manchester's One Piccadilly Gardens shows some of the range of transport choices available

Fig 3.12 Retaining the original contractor in a long-term management role is a feature of private finance initiative (PFI) schemes (such as at North Wiltshire District Council, pictured) and may have a wider application

Fig 3.10 Wessex Water provides a regular free bus link to Bath city centre to discourage car travel

CHAPTER 04

Lessons from the case studies
— practical steps to achieving better places to work

- **The planning stage**
- **The design and development stage**
- **The operation stage**

The case studies reveal a number of lessons about process – the key steps that need to be taken by the various players to increase the chances of producing a workplace that succeeds in a number of ways.

This set of lessons is presented below, grouped into three phases: planning, design and development, and operation.

4.1 The planning stage

Local planning authorities (LPAs) are core to the delivery of better places to work. While having to operate within the confines of the market and with a range of other actors, LPAs should be a proactive force. This involves a range of activities, including:

- forecasting and assessing the demand;
- including adequate sites for workplaces in local development frameworks, with a focus on both quality and quantity;
- including policies in local development frameworks that encourage quality workplaces and, if relevant, particular sectors, with the policy backed up by supplementary planning documents, where appropriate;
- working with other agencies to prepare suitable sites for workplace development, including remediating brownfield sites and providing infrastructure;
- preparing development briefs or masterplans for employment sites, sometimes working with landowners or developers to do so;
- entering into pre-application discussions with employers and developers to help ensure that the needs and expectations of both parties are met;
- encouraging developers and designers to actively involve local communities as early as possible in the decision-making process;
- assisting employers to find sites that meet their needs;
- signposting the relevant design and planning advice to applicants;
- encouraging innovation within the parameters of the planning system;
- with other agencies, providing funding and other support;
- imposing planning conditions and negotiating planning obligations that both accentuate the positive and mitigate the negative.

Fig 4.1 High Wycombe District Council recommended alternative sites to Ercol when they were seeking to relocate from local premises that had grown unsuitable

Fig 4.2 Newcastle City Council promoted development for regeneration purposes of the area around One Central Square

4.2 The design and development stage

Drawing on lessons from the case studies, there are a number of steps that all involved can usefully take during the design and development phase. These include:

- **Involve all the stakeholders at the earliest opportunity** The design of a successful workplace necessitates close working from the outset with as many key people and organisations as is practical. It is expected that the developer, employer/occupier, local planning authority, design team, local community, Regional Development Agency and funding agencies will all have something to contribute to the process, and early involvement not only smoothes the planning process but will result in a better outcome.

Fig 4.4 Public consultation prior to the development of Chiswick Park resulted in public access being granted to its green spaces and lake

Fig 4.3 The Piccadilly Partnership, involving Argent (the developer), Manchester City Council, the Greater Manchester Passenger Transport Executive and other stakeholders, prepared a framework for the development of the area around One Piccadilly Gardens

● **Consult the experts** No organisations, including developers, local planning authorities and designers, have all the skills or knowledge necessary to produce a high-quality workplace alone. But they can be accessed. CABE is a logical starting point, although other specialist expert advice may also be required.

● **Be prepared to take risks** Speculative development is a risky business, and some of the most interesting and successful schemes often carry the least certainty. However, as examples show, developers who invest in good design reap significant benefits. Similarly, most local planning authorities should be proactively seeking high quality outcomes and this may imply taking short term risks for long term benefits.

Fig 4.7 Parabola Estates successfully developed One Central Square at a level of quality and rental value that was at odds with the prevailing market wisdom

Fig 4.5 The architects of the Wessex Water Operations Centre consulted the Building Research Establishment on energy efficiency

Fig 4.8 The Custard Factory's developer took a risk in providing space for a market sector that had little or no track record or proven demand in the city

Fig 4.6 Acoustic consultants succeeded in minimising the noise impact of production in the Ercol factory

● **Embrace good design to smooth the planning process** Good design in workplaces is important for many positive reasons. As outlined at the beginning of this guide, it is good for business and good for the local area. It should also be used to find solutions to the problems and issues that inevitably arise as a scheme progresses through the planning system.

● **Mix it up, open it up** Workplaces can be more than just a place of work. Open space, cafés, shops and leisure facilities with public access can contribute to local amenity as well as being attractive to employees. Alternatively, facilities can be provided for employees alone; but while this may make for a more comfortable place to work, it does not contribute to a wider mixed-use civic environment. Designing to accommodate varying kinds of tenants in office developments can create a more varied occupancy, and spread financial risk by being less reliant on one tenant or sector.

Fig 4.9 The loading bays in the 3663 depot have been internalised to reduce noise impact on its neighbours

Fig 4.12 One Piccadilly Place's space for largely independent retail and restaurant uses also provides an 'active frontage' onto the public space

Fig 4.10 Design and access solutions (such as undercroft parking) were implemented in response to local concerns about the intensification, transport and character implications of the development of Chiswick Park in a locality with predominantly retail and residential uses

Fig 4.11 The exceptional ecologically-led design and traffic management initiatives overcame objections to the Wessex Water Operations Centre's move to an Area of Outstanding Natural Beauty with limited transport capacity

Fig 4.13 A café and showering and changing facilities are provided at North Wiltshire District Council's offices

Fig 4.14 The developer and its architects carefully and deliberately created Chiswick Park as a different kind of workplace, with strong design and branding throughout

● **Differentiate** To varying extents, all of the case studies of better places to work differentiate themselves from the competition. This is done in terms of design, landscaping and the inclusion of public art, for example. Differentiation does not just make commercial sense, it also brings character to an area from a land use that is too often lacking in imagination.

Fig 4.15 The Custard Factory, with its public spaces, public art, sculpture and unusual use of colour on buildings, has become a visitor destination as well as a place of work

Fig 4.16 One Central Square is set in well landscaped public realm, with a landmark sculpture on the edge of the site

4.3 The operation stage

According to the lessons from the case studies of better places to work, steps that all actors can usefully take during the operation or post-planning, design and development phase include:

- **Use good design as part of a marketing strategy** Effective marketing often goes beyond simply making potential occupiers aware of what is on offer. It is important to generate a buzz about a workplace. This could be creating an image of a place where like-minded businesses operate, where employees will enjoy coming to work and that impresses clients. Marketing should not be seen as a way of selling a low-grade product - rather design quality should be an integral part of the marketing strategy at all levels.

- **Manage soundly and creatively** The long-term sustainability of any development is, to a large extent, determined by the way it is managed and maintained. This incorporates a variety of operational tasks, from building and grounds maintenance through traffic and parking management to the provision of shared meeting spaces.

Fig 4.17 The strong branding, manifested in marketing, architecture, landscape design and management, is a key feature of Chiswick Park

Fig 4.19 Chiswick Park has adopted a 'service culture' of management greater than that found in many business parks

Fig 4.18 The Custard Factory has successfully nurtured a reputation as Birmingham's creative industries hub

Fig 4.20 The PFI arrangement means that the contractor is responsible for both the building and long-term management of North Wiltshire District Council's offices

CHAPTER 05

Annex A: Ten better places to work

Introduction

The case studies are presented in a way that outlines how each performs in relation to the most relevant principles of better places to work featured in Chapter 2. Where a development does not perform especially well against a particular principle, that principle is not included in the write-up. Each case study is introduced by a summary of key facts, including a contact from whom more information can be obtained. User's perspectives are also provided to show what makes each place special.

Capital One headquarters, Nottingham

Proving that corporate headquarters and call centres are successful city centre uses

Key facts

Date of development: 1998 and 2002 (2 phases)

Developer: Capital One

Local Planning Authority: Nottingham City Council

Lead designer: ORMS

Cost/contract value: £32 million

"The redevelopment has become a catalyst for regeneration of the whole station district."

Building Magazine, 2000

Key success factors

● Successful re-use of redundant building and brownfield site.
● Easy access to sustainable journey to work modes and to local shopping.
● Regeneration effect on local city centre facilities.
● Design quality enhances character of the area.

The principles

Ease of movement and legibility

The main messages of this case study revolve around its location. Being in Nottingham city centre, it is extremely well placed to take advantage of the main railway station (with a footbridge to the station platform bridge), the adjoining light rail stop, bus services and road connections. Pedestrian access is convenient to local shopping and amenities of the adjacent canal.

Character, quality and continuity

The site comprises two buildings, a converted print works (Trent House) and a new adjacent building on a brownfield site (Loxley House). The combined impact of the two contrasting buildings is very effective in forming an enclosing façade to the north side of Station Street. The formal symmetrical elevation of Trent House, with a traditional proportion of solid to void, contrasts markedly with the fully glazed frontages of Loxley House.

The site has had a regeneration effect on a peripheral city centre location, making use of a vacant brownfield site and a redundant production building sited within a Conservation Area. The aims of the local planning authority were largely met – appropriate scale, some enhancement of the canal, and potential for future connection to the north side of the canal when development there is complete. The canal side has been landscaped and a terrace provided, accessed from the café, sited to provide an active ground floor addressing the canal, thus enhancing the wider public realm.

Diversity

Capital One's 2,500 employees on site benefit from being in the heart of the city and the facilities it offers, while the city benefits from a major employment site in a quarter formerly in need of regeneration. As well as surrounding city centre uses,

Maps on Tap V.2.0, ODPM. Crown copyright reserved, 2003. O S Licence 100041331

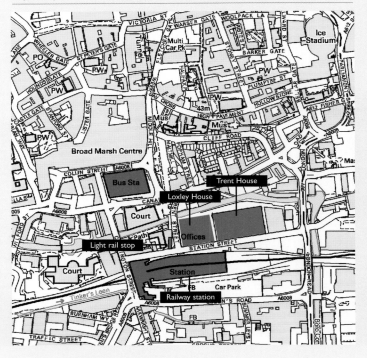

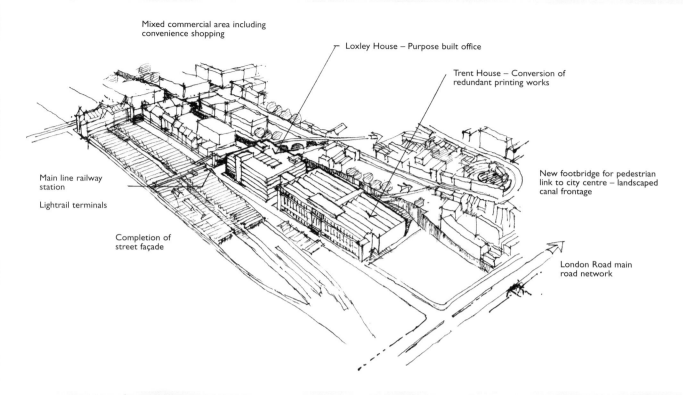

Mixed commercial area including convenience shopping

Loxley House – Purpose built office

Trent House – Conversion of redundant printing works

Main line railway station

Lightrail terminals

Completion of street façade

New footbridge for pedestrian link to city centre – landscaped canal frontage

London Road main road network

Fig A1.1 Plan of Capitol One headquarters, Nottingham

employees benefit from on-site facilities, including restaurants, coffee bars, games rooms, a shop and dry cleaning facilities.

Sustainability

Both buildings incorporate a number of environmentally considerate features including heating powered by a local recycled energy plant, aerated water and motion-sensitive lighting.

There is limited on-site parking, an active decision in line with the City Council planning guidelines, and only one in eight of the workforce travels to work by car. This is supported by Capital One offering associates interest-free loans for bus and train season tickets, access to on-line bus and train timetables,

and the provision of undercover secure cycle racks, showers and lockers.

Adaptability

Both buildings on site achieve large floor plates suitable for open plan offices and for flexibility in sub-leasing if required.

Fig A1.2 The neighbouring light rail station provides access to just one of the transport modes afforded by a city centre location

Fig A1.3 Loxley House enhances the street by completing the façade

Chiswick Park, London

A high-quality, well managed, well connected office park

Key facts

Date of completion: Phase 1: 2001; Phase 2: 2002
Developer: Stanhope plc
Local Planning Authority: London Borough of Hounslow
Lead designer: Richard Rogers Partnership
Cost/contract value: £115 million

"Churn here is very low. It's hard to lose people from good quality space."

Manager, occupying property company

"The environment is having a positive effect on our staff. People can unwind in the environment. We were expecting a 10-20% loss of staff with the move but it didn't happen."

Manager, occupying media company

Maps on Tap V.2.0, ODPM. Crown copyright reserved, 2003. O S Licence 100041331

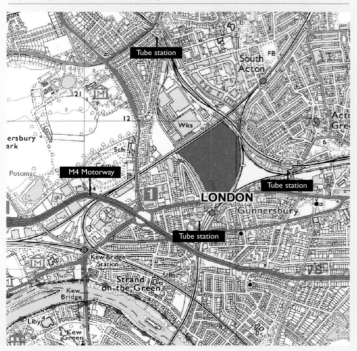

Key success factors

- The thoughtfulness and quality of the design, in terms of buildings, landscaping and materials, together with attention to detail, has created a high-quality workplace.
- The buildings offer a flexible, comfortable, well designed place to work.
- The external environment is designed to a high quality, and offers a pleasant environment for both users of the building and the public.
- The management and services offered are of a level above those normally provided.

The principles

Ease of movement and legibility

The park is located in a highly accessible position just off Chiswick High Street. Gunnersbury, Chiswick Park and Acton Town Underground stations and Kew Bridge and Acton South overground stations are all within walking distance, as are bus stops serving routes along Chiswick High Road towards Shepherds Bush and Hammersmith. The Chiswick roundabout at the end of the M4, and the north and south circular roads - giving easy access to Heathrow and the rest of London - is 500 m from the site. The next phase of development will enhance links to public transport. There is a car parking ratio of 1 space: 1,000 sq ft.

Character, quality and continuity

Phases 1 and 2 of Chiswick Park comprise six 4-storey office buildings of a similar design (steel structure with large glazed areas) and size (approx. 100,000 sq ft), in a landscaped setting with a pedestrianised avenue with a 2-tier lake between the buildings. A design objective was to keep cars away from the front of the buildings, avoiding the car-dominated environments of many office parks.

The quality of design and layout is exceptional; the materials, transparency and exposed structural devices provide visual interest to the simple rectangular forms of the buildings.

Diversity

Following the public consultation, done as part of the planning process, the developer was encouraged to open the site to the public, allowing them to use the footpaths and green areas surrounding the central lake. The mix of activities and uses on the site was achieved through the provision of amenities such as retail, a café and a gym – all provided on site and accessible for public use. These add to the vitality of the development as a workplace and increase the social contact between users.

Twenty-four hour public access contributes to the site's vitality and also helps in security terms by creating natural surveillance and maintaining activity throughout the day.

Management

A 'service culture' has been adopted in terms of management of the building, using a combination of strong branding (including the use of design) and a programme of activities and events that goes beyond the level of service normally offered in business parks. There is an Events Square – a multipurpose events area, hosting activities, sports, games and live entertainment – and a dedicated extranet for tenants, offering dry cleaning, photo service and delivery of groceries.

Fig A1.4 A commitment to design quality is central to Chiswick Park being recognised as a good place to work, with the benefits to occupiers and developer that brings

Fig A1.5 Simple branded signage makes the site highly legible

Fig A1.6 A strong public realm, with the water and soft landscaping, provides an interesting contrast to the predominantly glass and steel buildings

The Custard Factory, Birmingham

A vibrant mixed-use development that is much more than just a workplace

Key facts

Date of development: 1990 onwards
Developer: Bennie Gray
Local Planning Authority: Birmingham City Council
Lead designer: Glenn Howells Architects
Cost/contract value: Phase 1: £2 million, phase 2: £7 million

"This is a community that inspires and supports each other to ensure that every venture leads to success. It's great to be working in what is fast becoming the media centre of Birmingham."

Occupier, media consultancy

Key success factors

- Catalyst for the regeneration of Digbeth as the focus of the media and creative industries in Birmingham.
- The vision of the developer backed by supportive council policies.
- The imaginative re-use of redundant buildings and the spaces between them.
- The provision of accommodation attractive to a particular niche occupier.

The principles

Ease of movement and legibility

The Custard Factory is in the centre of Birmingham's urban area, around ³/₄ km to the south-east of the central city shopping area, and a short walk from the Bullring. It is less than 1 km from the central Birmingham rail stations, and four bus routes serve the site. The site is easily accessible by road networks in and around Birmingham.

Character, quality and continuity

The development occurred in two phases, in total hosting over 200 units of varying sizes, some of which were reserved for the use of artists' studios. Public spaces, public art, sculpture and the use of colour on buildings give character and identity to the development. The current mix of offices, studios, workshops and retail give the area vitality and life beyond standard office hours.

Diversity

In the late 1980s, Birmingham City Council was seeking to diversify its city centre economy, specifically by pursuing the development of the cultural industries sector. Digbeth was identified as a possible location for the creative industries, and planning and economic policy were formed to help achieve this aim. The 'Eastside' area, focused around the Custard Factory, has been identified by the Council as an area of mixed use, including residential, which will further repopulate and regenerate the area. Soon, a critical mass of such enterprises developed and additional facilities added value to the Custard Factory, such as a bar, galleries, nightclubs, shops and improvements to the public realm.

Maps on Tap V.2.0, ODPM. Crown copyright reserved, 2003. O S Licence 100041331

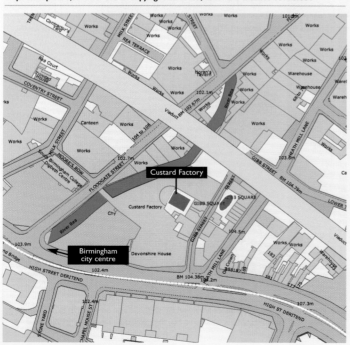

Fig A1.7 A sense of community is encouraged by the use of public and communal space within the development

The Custard Factory has indeed been a catalyst for the regeneration of the whole Digbeth area, as activity spreads beyond the confines of the site. Digbeth High Street is becoming populated by more people-friendly uses than previously as shops, cafés and a further education college open. The Council are encouraging this through improvements to the public realm and pedestrian environment. This is having the effect of expanding the city centre outwards from its traditional core, linking the Digbeth area with the recently regenerated Bullring area.

Management

Small units are available at short lets that have encouraged the development of small enterprise. Businesses have had the advantage of being located in close proximity, allowing interaction and networking to take place. Rooms and venue space can be hired as required (hourly, daily, weekly space available). There is an on-site advisor, available free of charge to tenants, to advise on funding opportunities and business development.

Fig A1.8 As the Custard Factory has increased in size the critical mass created has allowed more cafés, bars and retail units to open, and it is becoming a destination for people in the city beyond its role as a place of work

Fig A1.9 The former factory building has proved to be an excellent host of studio space for the creative industries

Ercol Factory, Princes Risborough, Buckinghamshire

A modern factory in a sensitive location of neighbouring residents and woodland

Key facts

Date of development: 2002

Developer: Ercol Holdings Ltd

Local Planning Authority: High Wycombe District Council

Lead designer: Horden Cherry Lee

Cost/contract value: £11.5 million

"The light, transparency and space the building offers is a real advantage. Everyone can see everyone, and getting around the site is far easier than in the previous site. Staff are very happy with the building, as am I."

Lucia Ercolani, Director

Key success factors

- Siting adjacent to the train station was fundemental to the selection of the site.
- Planners involvement in relocating this important local business from an inappropriate site to a better location within the area, reducing disruption for employees.
- Use of a brownfield site to continue traditional regional industry.
- Good standard of emissions control including effective noise suppression.
- Energy conservation measures, such as using waste heat from incinerator for water heating and process steam.

The principles

Ease of movement and legibility

The site is on the fringe of Princes Risborough adjoining rural and residential uses, through which the entrance road passes. The building exists as sole occupant of the site but further development is proposed. Car parking space is provided with this in mind. As is common in largely rural districts, the majority of staff use cars for journeys to work; the remainder walk, cycle or use the train, there being a station nearby.

Character, quality and continuity

The building has successfully integrated 160,000 sq ft of factory floor space, offices, and a large showroom. The factory is a clean, uncluttered and elegant design standing alone in a wooded setting. The open framing signifies the approach to the entrance from the car park at the front of the building. Thereafter, there is a clear sequence of reception, showroom, stairs to offices and, beyond that, the factory floor, all of which can be seen one from another.

Diversity

This is a modern production facility that sits successfully in a non-industrial estate location. Noise suppression was a key issue as there had been numerous complaints at the previous location. The reduction of noise was achieved with the advice of acoustic consultants and involved the use of perforated internal lining, 160 mm mineral wool insulation of the external cladding, acoustic louvres over space containing filter units (open to air to avoid explosion) and the housing of extract

Maps on Tap V.2.0, ODPM. Crown copyright reserved, 2003. O S Licence 100041331

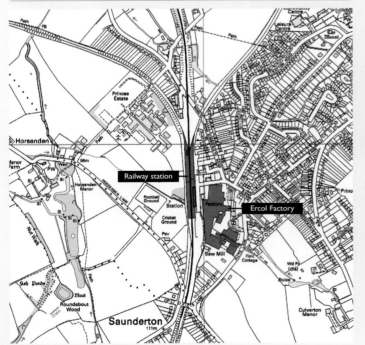

Fig A1.10 The factory floor has natural light from roof lights and continuous glazing the full length of the east side, providing external views

Fig A1.11 A modern building sitting unobtrusively in its rural environment

fans in a masonry enclosure. Emissions from the dust incinerator were reduced by burning at very high temperature with residue (usable potash) of only about two cubic metres per month.

Sustainability

The building is of special interest in suppressing emissions and minimising impact on the local residential areas. The extensive production area has all waste material extracted and incinerated with the heat used for hot water and steam.

Fig A1.12 The simple rectangular shape has been achieved by enclosing the normally obtrusive dust extraction equipment within the structure

North Wiltshire District Council, Chippenham

An environmentally intelligent local authority office that promotes the Council's vision of more open and democratic local government.

Key facts

Date of development:	2001
Developer:	North Wiltshire District Council
Local Planning Authority:	North Wiltshire District Council
Lead designer:	David Kent Architects
Cost/contract value:	£9.8 million

"The move to the new offices has changed office accommodation from being something which the staff continually complained about – rightly – to one which in our recent staff seminars was identified as being one of the key things that staff valued about working for us. Not bad when we also achieved substantial cash savings from the move."

Bob Marshall, Chief Executive, NWDC

Key success factors

- Demonstrates a wide range of the principles of better places to work.
- Particularly strong on location and associated sustainability issues.
- Long-term management commitment by the PFI contractors.
- Design responds well to contextual issues, such as slopes and the river.

The principles

Ease of movement and legibility

Council staff have been brought together from six dispersed sites into a single town centre location, close to public transport and shopping facilities. The offices are located very close to an off-road National Cycle Network route running along the river, and cycling is a popular option in the summer when the secure cycle parking area is usually full. Chippenham rail station is a short walk away.

Character, quality and continuity

Reflecting the nature of the Council's operations, the creation of a new single Council building in Chippenham offered the opportunity to promote the public-sector service purpose of the Council, and endorse a more open local government through the structure of the building. A single building where all functions were consolidated allowed a more accessible face to the public to be created and the means to increase interaction and communication between staff, councillors and the public.

Diversity

The site is accessible to the public who can use a riverside footpath and a footbridge across the river. Nearby, a sports centre, office and residential uses contribute to a mixed-use environment.

Sustainability

This project commenced with a Private Finance Initiative (PFI) bidding process. The brief was very broad and included site selection and emphasis on sustainability. The winning team selected the town centre Monkton Park site, in preference to lower cost greenfield sites on the edge of town. In spite of having to demolish the old council offices and relocate staff during building, the sustainability advantages were clear. The winning scheme also rated as excellent under BREEAM standards.

Maps on Tap V.2.0, ODPM. Crown copyright reserved, 2003. O S Licence 100041331

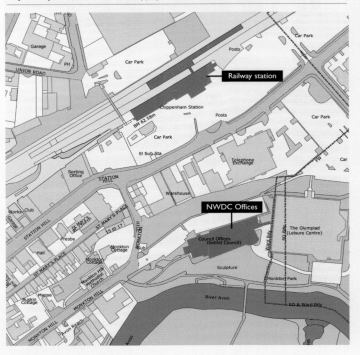

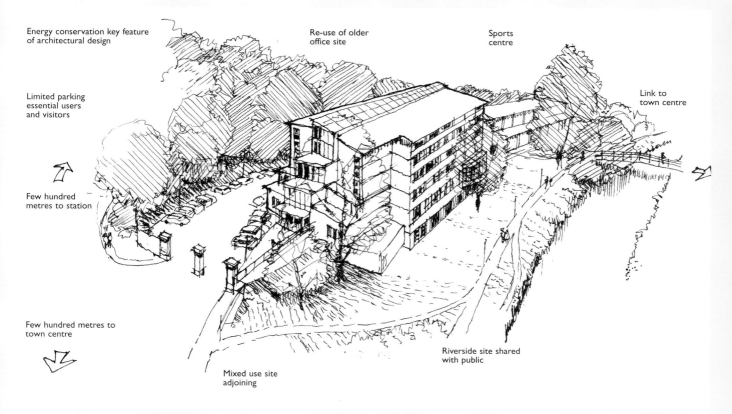

Energy conservation key feature
of architectural design

Re-use of older
office site

Sports
centre

Limited parking
essential users
and visitors

Link to
town centre

Few hundred
metres to station

Few hundred metres to
town centre

Riverside site shared
with public

Mixed use site
adjoining

Fig A1.13 Plan of North Wiltshire District Council offices, Chippenham, Wiltshire

Sustainability has been a high priority from the outset. Although it has a bright, modern and comfortable interior, the office uses only a fraction of the energy consumed by conventional heating, lighting and ventilation systems. A true 'intelligent' building, it regulates its own internal conditions, using automated windows in conjunction with prefabricated concrete coffered ceilings to smooth out peak summertime temperatures and keep the building cool. A central atrium and manually opening windows allow natural ventilation and maximise daylight in the building, while intelligent lighting dims lights when the sky is bright and turns them off when part of the office is unoccupied.

Management

Management is exercised on a long-term contract by a resident team from the PFI contractors. The building was completed in December 2001, ahead of schedule, and Jarvis now have a 25-year maintenance agreement and resident management staff.

Fig A1.14 The building relates well to the slopes, with two floors below the entrance level and three above

A1.15 The energy management system is designed to ensure that the building continues to operate efficiently throughout its life

One Central Square, Newcastle upon Tyne

A multi-occupancy office block that created a whole new market through the quality of its design

Key facts

Date of development: 1999

Developer: Parabola Estates

Local Planning Authority: Newcastle upon Tyne

Lead designer/architect: Carey Jones Architects

Cost/contract value: £8 million

"Relocating to One Central Square has given both a boost in morale to staff, as well as changing the status of the organisation. Customers like coming to the building, meaning we have less need to hire spaces elsewhere. It has set new standards for office design in the city."

**Andrew Dixon, Executive Director,
Arts Council England**

Key success factors

- Refurbishment of a disused 1930s sorting office into a high-quality office location.
- Catalyst for the regeneration of an underused site adjacent to the city centre.
- Very near to Newcastle Central Station with national and regional rail links, Metro services, and close to city centre facilities.
- Attention given to providing a quality working environment.

The principles

Ease of movement and legibility

Central Square is less than 250 m from Newcastle Central Station offering mainline routes and forming an interchange served by the majority of the city bus routes and the Metro system.

Character, quality and continuity

Focused around a large central atrium, One Central Square is an environmentally friendly building constructed in response to tenants and their employees' requirements. The developer appointed market researchers to ask prospective tenants what attributes contribute to a good place to work, which were analysed and fed into the design process. There was a desire from the start of the process to lift the quality of the development through aspects such as public art, additional amenity through the café, and how it performed as a place of work.

The office provides a number of places for interaction with clients, customers and colleagues, from offices, the shared conference and meeting facilities for formal events, and the use of the atrium and coffee bar for more informal interaction.

Design was a crucial factor in differentiating the development from the existing stock it was competing with in the market. This allowed for pre-lettings at rental values unheard of in Newcastle. A main reason for the building's commercial success, in what was an untested office location, has been the provision of a very different product in the local market. Setting a new standard for office developments in the city, One Central Square stimulated a previously dormant office market. As a result,

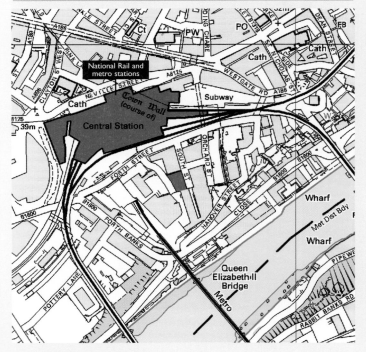

Maps on Tap V.2.0, ODPM. Crown copyright reserved, 2003. O S Licence 100041331

nearly 2 million sq ft of office space is in the pipeline. A second phase, Central Square South, has now been constructed, along the same principles of quality design, low running costs and built-in flexibility.

Diversity

Despite its central location, there was a lack of development in this part of the city, bounded by railway lines between the two growth areas of the quayside and the city centre. Development of this site coincided with the Council's realisation of the area's potential for commercial and residential development and creation of a City Centre Action Plan to enable it. The development has been a catalyst for the further regeneration and development of the area, including a second phase by the same developer.

Stephenson Quarter, as the area around Central Square has been labelled, is emerging as a truly mixed-use neighbourhood, with the activities of Parabola Estates the catalyst. In One Central Square itself, multi-occupancy was preferred over single occupancy, spreading risk, and improving the vitality and mix of the building. Users appreciate and value the mix of tenants, from commercial, arts and public sector organisations, as well as a popular café bar.

Sustainability

This is an environmentally friendly office building. Over 80% of the original building was retained, including the basement and window openings. Natural ventilation and lighting was used where possible, using orientation to supply light and air. It has a BREEAM rating of Excellent and won the Energy Efficiency category in the Royal Institution of Chartered Surveyors (RICS) Awards.

Adaptability

A 1930s postal sorting office, the building had become redundant by the early 1990s and lay vacant until it was acquired by Parabola Estates in 1998. The renovation has been designed to allow easy sub-division and flexibility to meet changing business requirements. The service cores are in the corners of the original building, leaving floorplates clear for sub-division.

A1.16 A 9.14 metre sculpture sits on the edge of the site, set in landscaping and public realm leading to the entrance of the building, giving the development identity and a sense of arrival

Fig A1.17 A large, glazed central atrium was constructed to contain the reception and a café

One Piccadilly Gardens, Manchester

A flagship speculative office development showing that modern Manchester means business

Key facts

Date of development:	2003
Developer:	Argent
Local Planning Authority:	Manchester City Council
Lead designer:	Allies and Morrison
Cost/contract value:	£22 million

"It has been adopted as a major meeting place by Manchester's teenagers…in warm weather the grass is barely seen for bodies. It's a huge success."

Building Design on the redevelopment of Piccadilly Gardens

"We were seeking a central location, offering high-quality office accommodation. One Piccadilly Gardens meets both these criteria."

Tim Keaney, Head of Europe, Bank of New York, tenant

Key success factors

● Flagship office scheme at the centre of the redevelopment of Piccadilly Gardens.
● Offers excellent public transport links to train, bus and Metrolink services, and is convenient for city centre facilities.
● Sets design standards for the regeneration of the 'Piccadilly Place' area to the east.
● The developer is a key member of the Piccadilly Partnership, working with Manchester City Council and the Greater Manchester Passenger Transport Executive to promote development in the Piccadilly area.

The principles

Ease of movement and legibility

The development benefits from excellent local, regional and national public transport links. Piccadilly Railway Station is less than half a mile away and Piccadilly Gardens is the main city centre bus and Metrolink interchange. There are also good pedestrian links to the city centre's main retail, leisure and commercial areas and road links to the motorway network.

Character, quality and continuity

Following a design competition, held by the developer in partnership with the local authority, architects were appointed with the brief of creating a high-quality office building to set the standard for future office development in the Piccadilly area.

Indeed, the building is an attractively designed office block, with generous glazing, clear elevations and good-quality detailing. Floor to ceiling glazing on each floor also contributes to the amount of natural light and offers views of the new public realm.

Fifteen million pounds were spent on revitalising the square, with the provision of 100 new semi-mature trees, plants, fountains, lighting, seating and public art. Piccadilly Gardens was previously a stigmatised piece of public realm, with problems of crime and anti-social behaviour in a poor environment, with particular problems after dark. Due to its location and prominence, the Manchester City Council identified its improvement as one of the key projects in the recent regeneration of the city centre, adopting the Piccadilly Development and Investment Framework in June 1997.

Maps on Tap V.2.0, ODPM. Crown copyright reserved, 2003. O S Licence 100041331

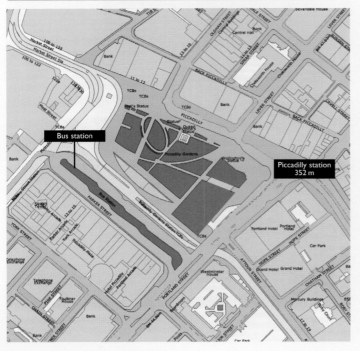

Fig A1.18 The regeneration of Piccadilly Gardens has been very successful. Anti-social behaviour that long haunted the area has been reduced, activity increased and the environment improved

Diversity

The active frontage to one side of the Square offers a mix of uses and increases vitality. These units have been selectively let to specialist uses such as a hairdressing salon, specialist bed company, upmarket bar and an organic food retailer. The developer felt it important to encourage local, independent companies to take up these leases - and were given 'softer' terms to encourage this - as they would have a greater interest in making the area work, and would help the development to be more distinctive than if common high street brands occupied the units.

Sustainability

The building has a 'very good' BREEAM rating, with showers and cycle parking, as well as the excellent public transport links that discourage users from travelling by car.

Adaptability

Large floorplates allow flexibility through being able to respond to varying demands in terms of size for potential occupiers.

Fig A1.19 A landmark office development plugged into the heart of the city

Management

The public-private Piccadilly Partnership has been formed to raise awareness of, and build upon, the huge public and private investment that has transformed the area in recent years and overcome the stigma associated with its past. This is done in a variety of ways, including: promoting Piccadilly as a brand; engaging transport providers in a dialogue about improving their services; and further improving the quality, management and maintenance of the public realm.

A1.20 Transport and those responsible for maintaining the public realm are engaged in the Piccadilly Partnership

The Printworks, Clitheroe, Lancashire

A well designed workplace in a rural context

Key facts

Date of development: 2002

Developer: North West Ltd

Local Planning Authority: Ribble Valley Borough Council

Lead designer: Levitt Bernstein

Cost/contract value: £1.6 million

"The Printworks provides an impressive setting for staff and clients. A good environment in which to work has contributed to the improved efficiency and productivity of our staff."

Jonathan Backhouse, Backhouse Jones Solicitors

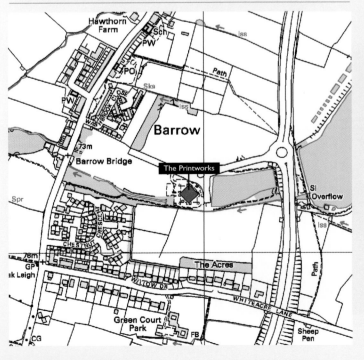

Maps on Tap V.2.0, ODPM. Crown copyright reserved, 2003. O S Licence 100041331

Key success factors

- Quality of building aided the retention of employers who may otherwise have moved out of the area.
- Despite the modest budget of the build, the quality achieved allowed higher than expected rents to be achieved.
- The use of the pond and landscaping provides a pleasant environment in which to work, which together with the design and materials used in the building, complement and capitalise on its rural setting.

The principles

Ease of movement and legibility

The property is in a rural setting approximately 10 km north of Blackburn and west of Burnley, on the western side of the A59 trunk road, on the Clitheroe/Whalley bypass. Junction 7 of the M65 is approximately 8 km to the south. Due to its rural location, the Printworks is only practically accessible by car. However, it is included as a case study in the recognition that workplaces may need to be sited in such locations, and in many rural locations, public transport access is not feasible.

Character, quality and continuity

The building is a simple shape: a square with a small central atrium and a pitched roof, with a glazed roof light over the atrium. It is built from a steel frame with timber cladding. The building fits well within its rural setting with timber cladding and a dark roof, assisting in a non-obtrusive appearance. Good tree planting and landscaping complement the design. Clear signage and the visual landmark of the atrium provide a clear, defined access to the site.

This case study shows that good design does not have to cost more. The cost of the build was kept economical while still retaining quality in its design, allowing an attractive, well-designed office building to be created in an area of limited demand and usually low rental values. Despite the modest budget, a good quality office building was achieved. The quality of the building allowed rental values beyond market expectations to be achieved.

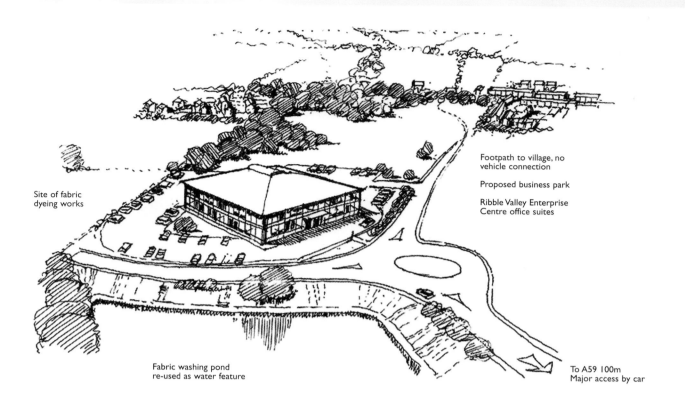

Site of fabric
dyeing works

Footpath to village, no
vehicle connection

Proposed business park

Ribble Valley Enterprise
Centre office suites

Fabric washing pond
re-used as water feature

To A59 100m
Major access by car

Fig A1.21 Plan of the Ribble Valley Enterprise Centre, Lancashire

The Printworks is the first phase of the Ribble Valley Enterprise Park. The Council faces issues relating to the retention of employment activities – many of the people who live in the area travel outside the authority to their places of work. The area has low unemployment levels, but also low average wages. The market has not traditionally provided for quality places of work that appeal to higher-end employers – who are more likely to be found in the urban areas of Manchester and Leeds.

Diversity

Further planned stages of the development include increasing the mix of uses on the site to include a hotel and conference centre, a bar/restaurant and a service station.

Fig A1.22 The entrance is clearly seen from the approach via a roundabout

A1.23 The quality of development was also improved through the attention given to landscaping, footpaths and the retention and use of the nearby water feature

3663, Langley Mill, Derbyshire

A well-located distribution depot with a regeneration role

Key facts

Date of development: August 2003

Developer: Miller Birch/3663 First for Foodservice

Local Planning Authority: Amber Valley Borough Council

Lead designer: KMG Partnership

Cost/contract value: £5.5 million

"The new depot fulfils our commercial requirements whilst providing a pleasant working environment for our people. We are especially proud of its aesthetic and functional design and its impact on its surroundings."

Steve Bonser, Depot General Manager

Maps on Tap V.2.0, ODPM. Crown copyright reserved, 2003. O S Licence 100041331

Key success factors

- First development in area designated for mixed business use.
- Regeneration effect in a town that has lost its older industries.
- Use of brownfield site following decontamination and involvement of East Midlands Development Agency.
- Good location for modal choice in travel to work.

The principles

Ease of movement and legibility

Location relative to the road network and motorway system is key to the development of any distribution depot. This, however, tends to encourage car use for journeys to work. In terms of the importance of the road access 3663 is no exception, but unusually for this type of workplace, is located in close proximity to public transport and town centre facilities.

Character, quality and continuity

Sited on a former contaminated brownfield site in a de-industrialising area and designed with some sensitivity, the depot is a positive presence in Langley Mill. As well as bringing much needed jobs, as the first building on a new business park, it has kick-started the physical regeneration of this part of Langley Mill.

Diversity

A distribution centre in an urban area is a potential bad neighbour. Heavy traffic access, 24-hours a day means that noise and air pollution can be major problems, but 3663 and their designers have taken steps to minimise impacts. The dispatch bay with lorry parking, for example, is less obtrusively positioned on the west side, partly screened by the office block and what in time will be a tree screen, and loading bays are 'internalised' by building configuration.

Sustainability

The building's principal environmental asset is its accessible location close to town centre facilities and the fact that it has been constructed on a remediated previously developed site.

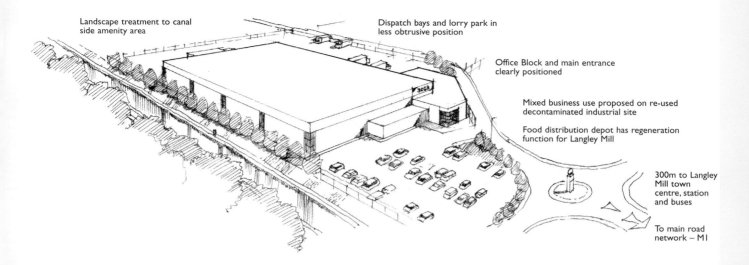

Landscape treatment to canal side amenity area

Dispatch bays and lorry park in less obtrusive position

Office Block and main entrance clearly positioned

Mixed business use proposed on re-used decontaminated industrial site

Food distribution depot has regeneration function for Langley Mill

300m to Langley Mill town centre, station and buses

To main road network – M1

Fig A1.24 Plan of 3663 Food Distribution Depot, Langley Mill, Derbyshire

Fig A1.25 The usual shortcomings of warehouse architecture are mitigated by siting offices and a reception area at the main public frontage

Fig A1.26 The frontage to the Erewash Canal has been animated with landscaping and, in part, glazed panels, thus adding amenity value

Wessex Water Operations Centre, Claverton Down

Environmental excellence making sound economic sense

Key facts

Date of development: 2000
Developer: Wessex Water
Local Planning Authority: Bath and East West Somerset
Lead designer: Bennetts Associates
Cost/contract value: £21.5 million

"The building has performed extremely well and done everything we wanted it to. It has fulfilled all our aspirations, and will be a benchmark of sustainability to other companies for many years to come. It stands as a clear demonstration that a modern commercial building can be created and operated on the principles of sustainability."

Colin Skellett, Chairman, Wessex Water

"Wessex Water has a very clear commitment as a company to environmental sustainability, and it is very fitting that those credentials are so clearly visible within the building which houses our operations centre. Not only the physical building, but many of the activities within it are also indicators of our sustainable principles. As well as the environmental benefits of the building, our operations centre has made a positive difference in terms of staff motivation and that's simply because it is a great place to work."

Mike Caple, Property Services Manager, Wessex Water

Maps on Tap V.2.0, ODPM. Crown copyright reserved, 2003. O S Licence 100041331

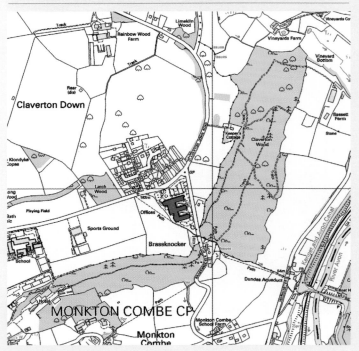

Key success factors

- Successful architectural design responding well to a sensitive site.
- Comprehensive energy conservation measures.
- An ongoing management commitment to providing a pleasant workplace.

The principles

Ease of movement and legibility

The development is in a rural location on the outskirts of Bath, approximately 3 km to the south-east of the city centre. The hilly surrounds and the rural location mean that regular public transport and cycling are not feasible options for the site's 580 workers to get to work. However Wessex Water has put schemes into place to provide alternatives to car use, such as a company bus service.

Character, quality and continuity

Although expansive, this low-rise building has been designed to be unobtrusive and is successful in responding to the slope, the aspect, views both inward and outward, and local landscape features. The building has a lightweight steel structure with exposed pre-cast concrete floor units with a high glazing ratio providing good levels of natural light. Views to the south (as far as Salisbury Plain) are in evidence from most interior spaces. Double-glazing and solar shading (using steel screens and aluminium louvres) are included to the south to prevent excessive heating. The rest of the building is clad in the local Bath stone, reflecting local history and character, and reducing the environmental impacts of transporting material from far afield.

Sustainability

This case study is successful in two main areas. First, the architectural response of the scheme in meeting the rigorous planning conditions arising from its sensitive wooded location and, second, in the way it has incorporated extensive energy conservation measures both within the design and subsequently in operational terms. This contribution to the sustainability agenda is important to counteract the negative effects arising from its position and limited public transport opportunities.

Energy conservation features within the building include solar panels, solar gain control, good natural light, cooling at night by controlled window opening, coffered concrete ceilings that are

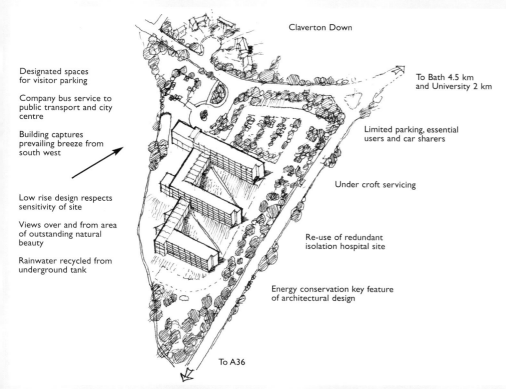

Claverton Down

Designated spaces
for visitor parking

Company bus service to
public transport and city
centre

Building captures
prevailing breeze from
south west

Low rise design respects
sensitivity of site

Views over and from area
of outstanding natural
beauty

Rainwater recycled from
underground tank

To Bath 4.5 km
and University 2 km

Limited parking, essential
users and car sharers

Under croft servicing

Re-use of redundant
isolation hospital site

Energy conservation key feature
of architectural design

To A36

Fig A1.27 Plan of Wessex Water Headquarters, Claverton Down, East Somerset

orientated to receive night breezes and there is a building management system. Rainwater is recycled for flushing WCs. Only the operations control room is air conditioned, other areas are naturally ventilated. The building has an 'Excellent' BREEAM rating.

The very high environmental specification generated a modest cost premium over a more standard office development. However, the building consumes less than a third of the energy required to power a standard air-conditioned headquarters office building, significantly reducing the operational costs. The building was considered to be the "greenest office building in the UK" on completion. This was much more than a design accolade – for the occupier, considering the whole life performance of the building in use was particularly cost-effective and made good business sense.

Because of location and the concern by management for sustainability, buses are operated at 15 minute intervals throughout the day, serving Bath city centre, the railway station, bus station and the park & ride facility. These buses have bicycle racks. In addition, the company has acquired a building next to the railway station that is intended to serve as a staff waiting room.

Management

Wessex Water is aware that the standards of planning and management that have delivered the building to this stage must continue if the building's performance is to be maintained, and have appointed three facilities managers. The role of the Facilities Department is to define and explain the building's environmental targets to all of its occupants to encourage their support and involvement.

Fig A1.28 The Operations Centre sits within an Area of Outstanding Natural Beauty, so design measures, such as the building being of only two storeys, terraced on the south facing slope, and careful choice of materials minimise visual impact and integrate the building into its surroundings

Fig A1.29 Despite the rural location, car parking is restricted to essential users or members of a car-share scheme

Appendix I

Further reading and references

- The Bartlett School of Planning, UCL for CABE and BCO (2004) *Offices, value, design: economic value, valuation, and the design quality of office development* (CABE and the British Council for Offices)

- British Council for Offices (2000) *BCO Guide 2000: best practice in the specification for offices*

- British Council for Offices (2004) *Improving planning for offices: the perfect local authority*

- CABE (2002) *The value of good design*, www.cabe.org.uk

- DETR & CABE (2000), *By design: urban design in the planning system: towards better practice*

- DoE (2001) *Planning policy guidance 4: industrial, commercial development and small firms*

- Llewelyn Davies for English Partnerships (2000), *The urban design compendium*

- Llewelyn Davies for the South Yorkshire Objective I Programme (2003) *Better places to work in South Yorkshire*

- ODPM (2203) Commercial and Industrial Floorspaces and Ratable Value Statistics, November. Available at www. odpm.gov.uk/stellent/groups/odpm/planning/documents/page/odpm_plan_025920.pdf

- CABE and BCO (2005), *The impact of office design on business performance*

Appendix 2

Further information

The following organisations are useful sources of additional information

Commission for Architecture and the Built Environment
www.cabe.org.uk

British Council for Offices
www.bco.org.uk

Office of the Deputy Prime Minister
www.odpm.gov.uk

British Property Federation
www.bpf.org.uk

Appendix 3

Acknowledgments

Project team

Better places to work was prepared by Llewelyn Davies Yeang (Ben Castell, Jonathan Moore, Keith Denham, Patrick Clarke and Sophie Medhurst) in association with Atisreal (Jeremy Edge, Rebecca Thevarokiam) on behalf of CABE.

Steering group

The Project Steering Group included representatives from CABE (Lee Scott, Esther Kurland and Stephen King) and ODPM (Alex Turner).

Sounding board

Further advice was received through a Sounding Board consisting of the following people: Paul Watson (Solihull Metropolitan Borough Council); Faraz Baber (British Property Federation); Simon Carne (Urban Initiatives); Andrew Chandler (Spacia Ltd); Richard Cutler (Arlington Securities Ltd); Ron German (Stanhope plc); Annie Hampson (Corporation of London); David Hoy (Diageo); Nigel Hughill (Chelsfield plc); Stephen Kelly (Watford Borough Council); Palmyra Kownack (British Property Federation); Wally Kumar (Development Securities); Richard Mead (IBM United Kingdom Ltd); Jon Muncaster (English Partnerships); Mark Rowlands (3663); Jonathan Whitehead (Royal Mail Property Holdings).

Image credits

The following people and organisations are gratefully acknowledged for supplying all the figures listed below.

- CABE: 1.2, 4.5, A1.3, A1.28

- David Gilbert at View Pictures, (Doxford International courtesy of Studio E Architects):
  Front cover, page 3, page 7, 2.4, 4.1, 4.7, A1.10, A1.11, A1.12

- Duncan Johnson
  Page 4, Page 19, 3.5, 4.14, A1.14, A1.15

- Keith Paisely
  Front cover, page 3, page 23, 4.2, A1.16, A1.17

- David Millington
  Front cover, page 3, 4.4, A1.19, A1.20

- Llewelyn Davies Yeang
  All other images in this publication

- Tom Scott
  3.1, page 31, A1.22, A1.23

- The ten location maps used in the chapter Case studies were obtained and reproduced with the kind permission of Maps on Tap, ODPM
  Maps on Tap V.2.0, OPDM. Crown copyright reserved, 2003. O S Licence 10004 1331